To Judy
on your 70th Birthday

Ma

Life Is All About How You Handle Plan B

ISBN: 978-1-59842-831-5

Wonderful Wacky Women.
Inspiring•Uplifting•Empowering

is a trademark of Suzy and Al Toronto. Used under license.

M and Blue Mountain Press are registered in U.S. Patent and Trademark Office. Certain trademarks are used under license.

Printed in China.
Second Printing: 2015

⊕ This book is printed on recycled paper.

This book is printed on paper that has been specially produced to be acid free (neutral pH) and contains no groundwood or unbleached pulp. It conforms with the requirements of the American National Standards Institute, Inc., so as to ensure that this book will last and be enjoyed by future generations.

Blue Mountain Arts, Inc.
P.O. Box 4549, Boulder, Colorado 80306

Life Is All About How You Handle Plan B

Suzy Toronto

Blue Mountain Press™
Boulder, Colorado

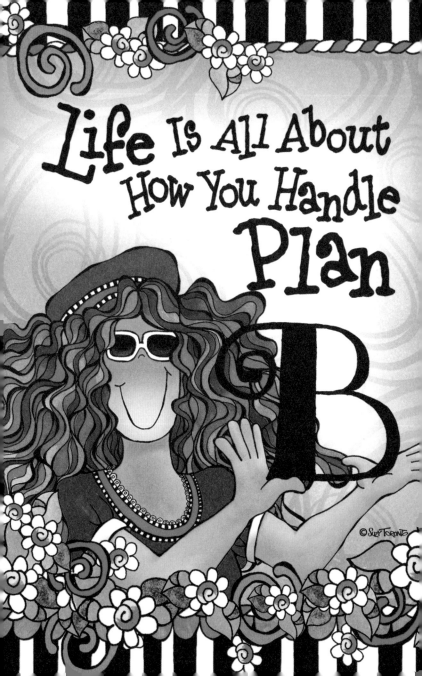

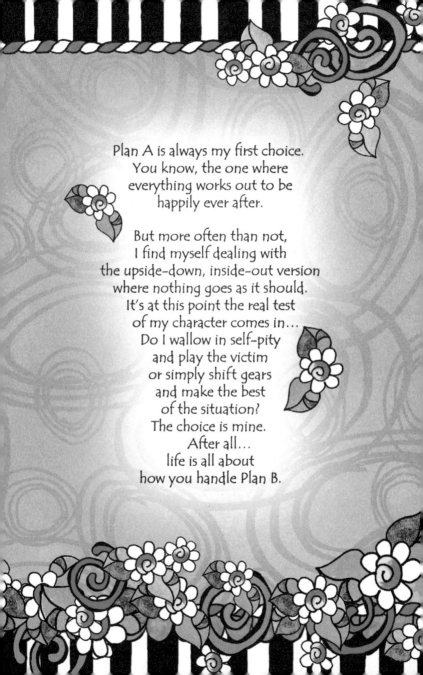

Plan A is always my first choice.
You know, the one where
everything works out to be
happily ever after.

But more often than not,
I find myself dealing with
the upside-down, inside-out version
where nothing goes as it should.
It's at this point the real test
of my character comes in...
Do I wallow in self-pity
and play the victim
or simply shift gears
and make the best
of the situation?
The choice is mine.
After all...
life is all about
how you handle Plan B.

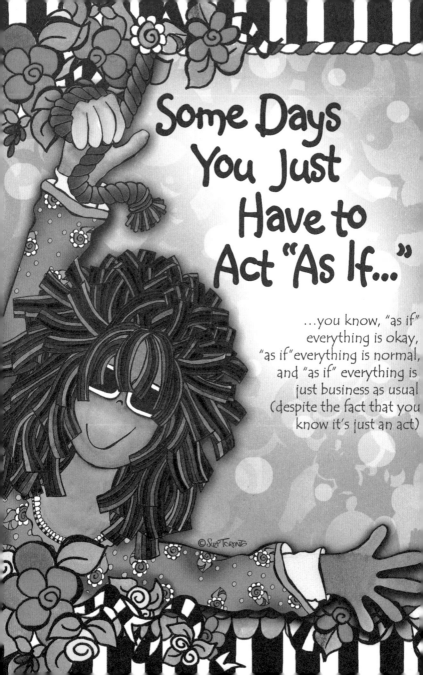

Some Days You Just Have to Act "As If..."

...you know, "as if" everything is okay, "as if" everything is normal, and "as if" everything is just business as usual (despite the fact that you know it's just an act)

©Suzy Toronto

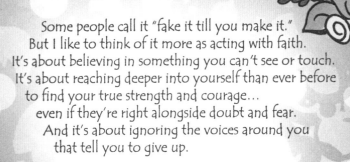

Some people call it "fake it till you make it."
But I like to think of it more as acting with faith.
It's about believing in something you can't see or touch.
It's about reaching deeper into yourself than ever before
to find your true strength and courage...
even if they're right alongside doubt and fear.
And it's about ignoring the voices around you
that tell you to give up.

Think of it this way:
What if just around the next corner
a shiny brass ring is waiting for you?
What if the rainbow's end is just around the bend,
its pot of gold emblazoned with your name?
What if you act "as if" for just one more minute?
This is not the time to wimp out and be a chicken.
This is the time to press forward with faith.
This is the time to put on your game face
and act "as if" nothing were impossible.
When you do, you will stand tall
with conviction and pride, knowing you have
finally created the life you've always imagined.

I know sometimes
Life
can be rough...

Everyone's life is full
of harrowing rapids
at times, and riding
life's currents is
part of the challenge.
Some days you may
seem to have more
than your share
of rough waters
and feel tested
to the limit.

The hardest part of all is that
the solution is up to you.
Will you sink or will you swim?
Will you curl up and play the victim,
or will you draw on that strength
deep down inside you
and start swimming
like there is no tomorrow?

Once you get started,
the journey will get easier
(even though you may have to
go through this scenario several
times before you make it to shore).
But with each stroke you take
you become stronger
and more resistant
to the next current
that comes your way.
Just remember...
you can do it.

© Suzy Toronto

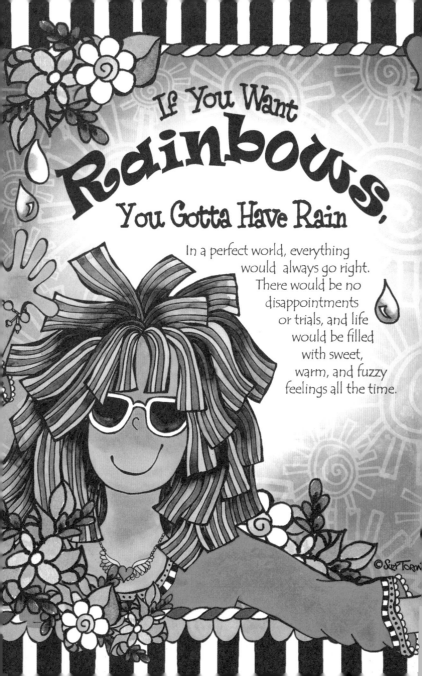

If You Want Rainbows,
You Gotta Have Rain

In a perfect world, everything would always go right. There would be no disappointments or trials, and life would be filled with sweet, warm, and fuzzy feelings all the time.

© Suzy Toronto

But how would we know if things were good
if we had no comparison?
Would we recognize the blessings in our lives
without having the opposite to compare them to?
Without the darkness,
would we appreciate the light?

Seems to me if we want rainbows, we gotta have rain.
The trick is to pull ourselves up by our bootstraps
and go out and look for puddles to play in,
recognize the tempest for what it is,
and train ourselves to look for the good
in every situation.
By overcoming our adversity,
we find the joy in everything.
So go on, go play in the rain!

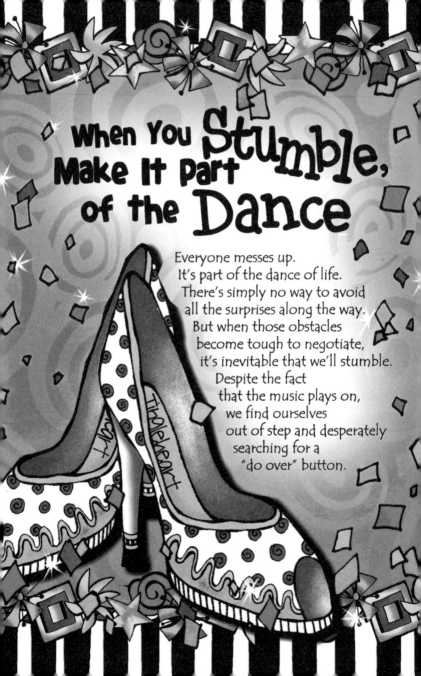

When You Stumble, Make It Part of the Dance

Everyone messes up.
It's part of the dance of life.
There's simply no way to avoid
all the surprises along the way.
But when those obstacles
become tough to negotiate,
it's inevitable that we'll stumble.
Despite the fact
that the music plays on,
we find ourselves
out of step and desperately
searching for a
"do over" button.

That's when creativity and adaptability
become our most valuable, lifesaving virtues.
They help us muster up the courage to carry on
and simply act as if it were all part of the show…
even though behind the scenes
our pride may have been battered and bruised.
Without offering apologies,
excuses, or explanations,
we discover that it's just a matter of
continuing onward with all our heart and soul
as if our lives depended on it.

So the next time you stumble, smile at the crowd,
kick up your heels, and dance a jig!
The moment you embrace it as your own,
no one will know it's not part of <u>your</u> dance.

©Suzy Toronto

Dare to Be Wacky...
Live a Life Worth
Loving

We all have it in us —
a free-spirited, wonderful, wacky
attitude that makes our lives
colorful, exciting, and fun.
It inspires us to write
our own wacky fairy tale,
filled with fascinating
characters, plenty
of action,
and plots that
twist and turn.

© Suzy Toronto

But sometimes we mistake that wild,
unbridled energy for chaos and confusion
and allow critics to cut out
the best scenes in our story.
The whole process stifles our passions
and dulls our sparkle, and we
no longer fully cherish our lives.
Well, not anymore!

This is the year, and now is the moment.
Rekindle your passions,
and multiply your talents.
Embrace your inner wackiness,
and redefine your world.
Stand up for something worth fighting for,
and confront the dragons of the world...
especially if they scare you.
Make a difference in someone's life...
in the process, you'll change your own.

Don't wait for "a better time."
It's your life and your story.
So dare to be wacky...
and truly live a life worth loving!

Don't Let Your Frame of Mind Frame You In

Have you ever felt like
dancing in a fountain?
Fully clothed?
In the middle of the day?
With people everywhere?
I've seen someone do it,
and the laughter and smiles
tell you in a minute
that the scene has just
made everyone's day.

Most of us have crazy thoughts like that,
but we don't act on them.
Our frame of mind frames us in.
It dampens our growth, stamps out our creativity,
and wreaks havoc with our imagination.

Daring to be wacky means
stepping out of our comfort zones,
taking a chance, and creating a life worth loving.
Sure, it's risky — but so what?
Being a wacky woman means following your heart.
You don't have to be obnoxious or extreme;
just be willing to step outside the box,
let go of your doubts, and grab hold of
the first opportunity that comes your way.
Take music lessons. Go back to school.
Make friends with an old rival.
Volunteer for charity. Run a race. Adopt a mutt.
Try out for a play. Join a yoga class.
The results will amaze you.
You're never too old, too young,
too rich, or too poor to just <u>do it</u>.
Ready? Set. Go!

© Suzy Toronto

Everyone wants to get ahead in this world,
but it's hard when people go about it in thoughtless ways.
They puff themselves up with hot air, seek attention and praise,
and end up stepping on whomever they can to get higher.
Many of us know what that feels like —
been there! done that! — and it's really not that much fun.

The fact is that the real rise to the top
is a lot easier than it sounds.
Just let go of the idea that you need to climb
somewhere or something, and concentrate
on lifting and inspiring others along their journey.
When you stop focusing on yourself,
you end up finding extraordinary joy
in watching others' dreams take flight.

And here's the best part.
In the process, they become
the "wind beneath our wings."
We effortlessly float to the top
and find ourselves soaring higher than ever before.
The ride is a blast, and the view is amazing.
So inspire, uplift, and empower others.
It is the secret to true and lasting greatness.

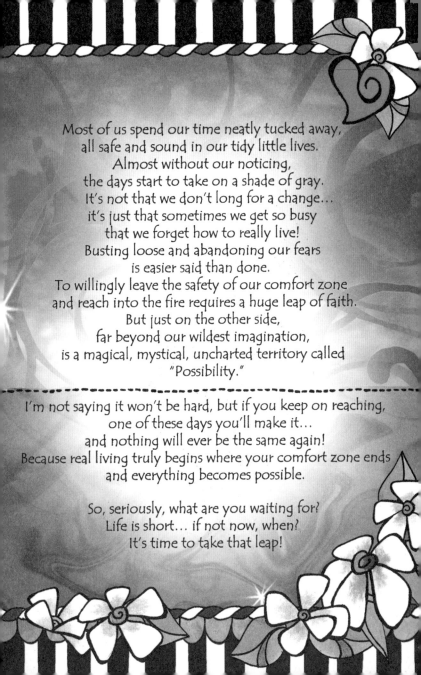

Most of us spend our time neatly tucked away,
all safe and sound in our tidy little lives.
Almost without our noticing,
the days start to take on a shade of gray.
It's not that we don't long for a change...
it's just that sometimes we get so busy
that we forget how to really live!
Busting loose and abandoning our fears
is easier said than done.
To willingly leave the safety of our comfort zone
and reach into the fire requires a huge leap of faith.
But just on the other side,
far beyond our wildest imagination,
is a magical, mystical, uncharted territory called
"Possibility."

I'm not saying it won't be hard, but if you keep on reaching,
one of these days you'll make it...
and nothing will ever be the same again!
Because real living truly begins where your comfort zone ends
and everything becomes possible.

So, seriously, what are you waiting for?
Life is short... if not now, when?
It's time to take that leap!

Epic Mistake

#5,372 That I Made on Purpo

I mess up a lot. And I'm not talking about little, unnoticeable flub I'm talking all-out spectacles to behold... epic stuff that legends are made o

But here is the secret that few people know — I make a lot of mistakes on purpose.

© Stef Toronto

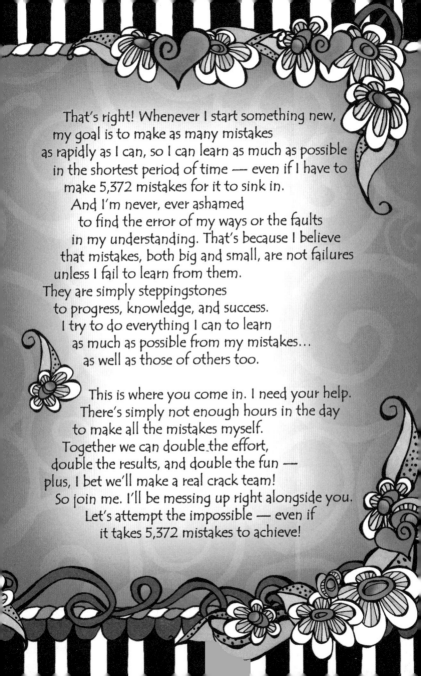

That's right! Whenever I start something new,
my goal is to make as many mistakes
as rapidly as I can, so I can learn as much as possible
in the shortest period of time — even if I have to
make 5,372 mistakes for it to sink in.
And I'm never, ever ashamed
to find the error of my ways or the faults
in my understanding. That's because I believe
that mistakes, both big and small, are not failures
unless I fail to learn from them.
They are simply steppingstones
to progress, knowledge, and success.
I try to do everything I can to learn
as much as possible from my mistakes...
as well as those of others too.

This is where you come in. I need your help.
There's simply not enough hours in the day
to make all the mistakes myself.
Together we can double the effort,
double the results, and double the fun —
plus, I bet we'll make a real crack team!
So join me. I'll be messing up right alongside you.
Let's attempt the impossible — even if
it takes 5,372 mistakes to achieve!

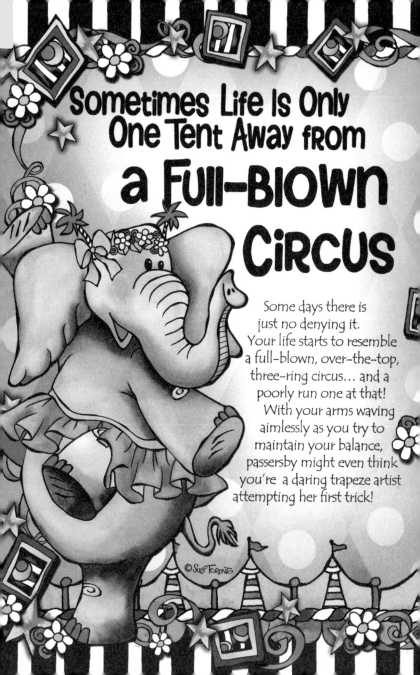

Sometimes Life Is Only One Tent Away from a Full-Blown Circus

Some days there is just no denying it. Your life starts to resemble a full-blown, over-the-top, three-ring circus… and a poorly run one at that! With your arms waving aimlessly as you try to maintain your balance, passersby might even think you're a daring trapeze artist attempting her first trick!

© Suzy Toronto

But guess what?
You are not alone.
Up and down your street,
around each corner,
and behind closed doors,
at some point most of us
have also had the same experience.

So if life is going to be a circus, rally your friends,
step right up, and make it the greatest show on earth...
the likes of which the world has never known.
Once you do, you'll find that your troubles are easier
when you embrace them with friends.
And if there happens to be an elephant
in the corner of the room,
just go ahead and introduce her
and let her perform!

So hoist up that last big tent,
march in the menagerie,
and let the show begin.
It's going to be
stupendous!

EAT SUNSHINE FOR BREAKFAST

and You'll Beam Radiantly All Day

If you're anything like me, a lot of days feel like the deck is stacked against you. You try to plow through the piles of stuff that seem to have mysteriously appeared while you slept and fight to catch your breath through it all... or at the very least catch a glimpse of the light at the end of the tunnel.

© Suzy Toronto

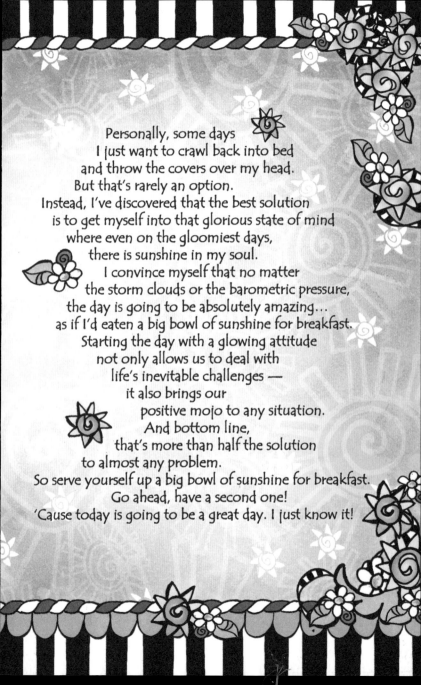

Personally, some days
I just want to crawl back into bed
and throw the covers over my head.
But that's rarely an option.
Instead, I've discovered that the best solution
is to get myself into that glorious state of mind
where even on the gloomiest days,
there is sunshine in my soul.
I convince myself that no matter
the storm clouds or the barometric pressure,
the day is going to be absolutely amazing...
as if I'd eaten a big bowl of sunshine for breakfast.
Starting the day with a glowing attitude
not only allows us to deal with
life's inevitable challenges —
it also brings our
positive mojo to any situation.
And bottom line,
that's more than half the solution
to almost any problem.
So serve yourself up a big bowl of sunshine for breakfast.
Go ahead, have a second one!
'Cause today is going to be a great day. I just know it!

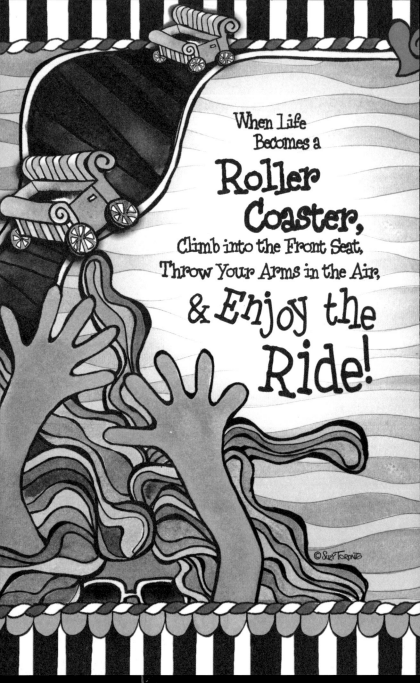

Life is full of ups and downs.
If you're anything like me,
more than once you've prayed to God
to take away some of the low spots.

If I had only realized that
the experience I was trying to avoid
was actually a life-altering opportunity
that shaped me into the woman I am today,
I would have yelled, "Hit me with your best shot!"

Knowing this after the fact didn't make it any easier,
but looking back I realize I am much better now
for having endured it. Besides, I'd never have realized
how high I have gotten without the perspective
of how low I had been.

The real lesson to be learned is that we
need to face our challenges head-on…
with grace, style, and conviction.

So the next time your life
starts to resemble a roller coaster,
climb into the front seat,
throw your arms in the air,
and enjoy the ride!

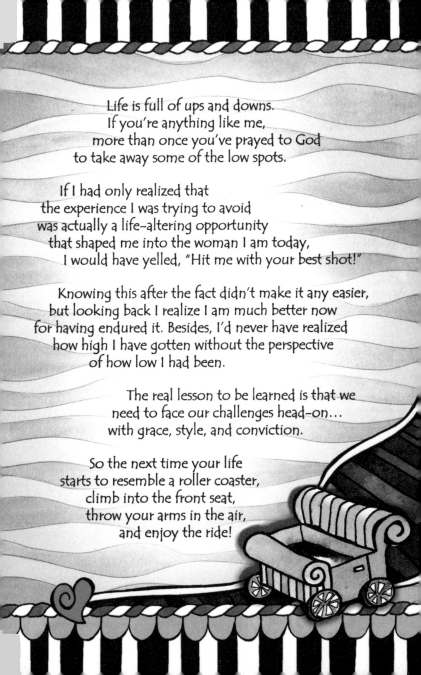

Life is all about give and take.
But some issues can't be compromised.
When the situation calls
for drastic and dramatic measures,
you have to draw a line in the sand,
climb up on a soapbox,
and protect the hill you're willing to die on.

It's not easy...
anything worth fighting for never is.
But the most noble thing you can do
is stand up for what is right, no matter the cost.

The problem is your voice can drown
amid the roar of the masses.
Once in a while you have to stomp your feet,
scream at the top of your lungs,
and throw a few lightning bolts to be heard.

Never underestimate the power of a "hissie fit."

Yeah, I'm a big girl.
And when I need to, I can rise to any occasion.
I put on my "I can do anything" face,
jump in over my head,
and learn to swim on the way up.

But don't be fooled.
I struggle just as much as anyone.
Underneath my can-do facade,
I'm shaking in my boots,
and it's really hard to get my
sparkling and effervescent personality
to twinkle and shine!
So if I get a little testy with you,
don't take it personally.
And please… don't tell me to
put on my big-girl panties
and deal with it.

I am wearing 'em,
but they're starting
to bunch, OK!?

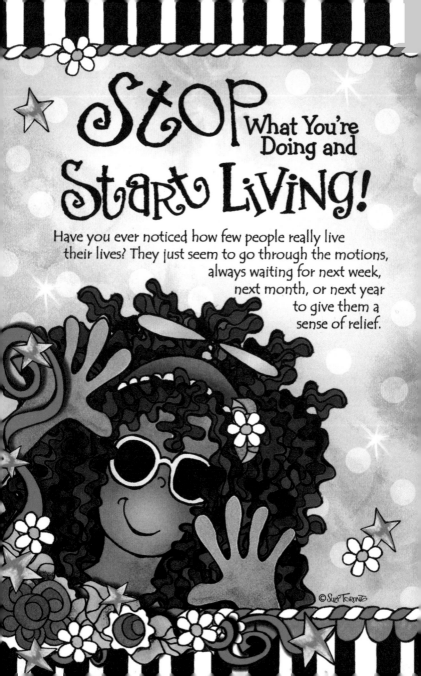

StOP What You're Doing and Start LiViNG!

Have you ever noticed how few people really live
their lives? They just seem to go through the motions,
always waiting for next week,
next month, or next year
to give them a
sense of relief.

© Suzy Toronto

It's a trap that's far too easy to fall into.
(Oh yeah, I know you've been there;
I was the wild-haired, wacky woman
right next to you, running around
like a chicken with her head cut off.)
So right this very second,
stop what you're doing and start living.
Let go of the chaos and choose to
fully embrace every minute of your life.
Proclaim today as <u>your</u> day and this
very instant as your moment for the taking.
This day will never come again.
Next week will still come,
deadlines will fly by,
and appointments will come and go,
but by tomorrow…
today will be gone forever.

So take a deep breath, let go, and LIVE!

Do not take the advice
of that old sage
and wait until you can
"walk confidently
in the direction of your dreams."
If you do, you'll never take the first step.
Instead, leap and learn to fly on the way down.
(And for heaven's sake, don't wait
until you lose ten pounds!)

Now is the time to jump in with both feet...
arms flailing, hair flying, and screaming at
the top of your lungs, "I can do this!"

You don't have to believe it...
you just have to do it.

Start now!

Ten Things to Remember for a Wonderful Wacky Life

 # 10 Think big. If that doesn't work, think bigger.

 # 9 If you want rainbows, you gotta have rain.

 # 8 When life becomes a roller coaster, climb into the front seat, throw your arms in the air, and enjoy the ride.

 # 7 Inches, ages, and sizes don't tell you anything about the amazing woman inside.

 # 6 When life gives you a second chance, take it.

© Suzy Toronto

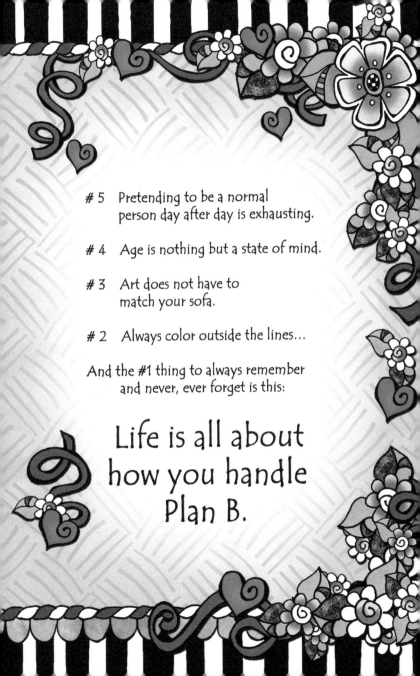

5   Pretending to be a normal
         person day after day is exhausting.

4   Age is nothing but a state of mind.

3   Art does not have to
         match your sofa.

2   Always color outside the lines...

And the #1 thing to always remember
         and never, ever forget is this:

Life is all about
how you handle
Plan B.

About the Author

So this is me… I'm a tad wacky and just shy of crazy. I'm fiftysomething and live in the sleepy village of Tangerine, Florida, with my husband, Al, and a big, goofy dog named Lucy. And because life wasn't crazy enough, my eightysomething-year-old parents live with us too. (In my home, the nuts don't fall far from the tree!) I eat far too much chocolate, and I drink sparkling water by the gallon. I practice yoga, ride a little red scooter, and go to the beach every chance I get. I have five grown children and over a dozen grandkids who love me as much as I adore them. I teach them to dip their French fries in their chocolate shakes and to make up any old words to the tunes they like. But most of all, I teach them to never, ever color inside the lines. This is the Wild Wacky Wonderful life I lead, and I wouldn't have it any other way. Welcome to my world!

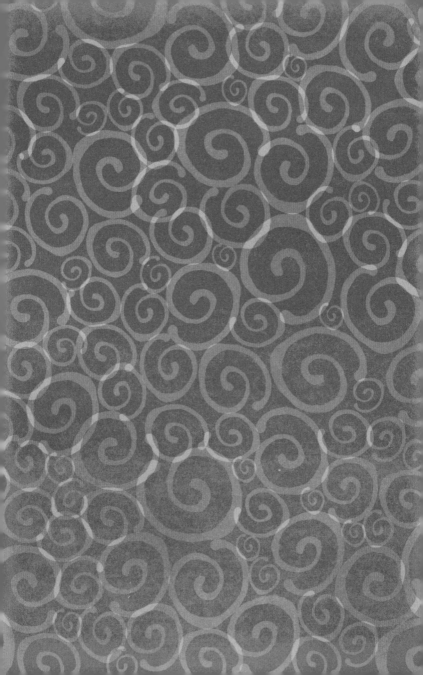